First Facts® PREDATOR PROFILES

KILLER WHALES

- BUILT FOR THE HUNT -

by Christine Zuchora-Walske

Consultant: Dr. Jackie Gai, DVM
Wildlife Veterinarian

CAPSTONE PRESS
a capstone imprint

First Facts are published by Capstone Press,
1710 Roe Crest Drive, North Mankato, Minnesota 56003
www.capstonepub.com

Library of Congress Cataloging-in-Publication Data
Zuchora-Walske, Christine, author.
Killer whales: built for the hunt / by Christine Zuchora-Walske.
pages cm. — (First facts. Predator profiles)
Summary: "Informative, engaging text and vivid photos introduce readers to the predatory lives of killer whales"—Provided by publisher.
Audience: Ages 6-9.
Audience: K to grade 3.
Includes bibliographical references and index.
ISBN 978-1-4914-5042-0 (library binding)
ISBN 978-1-4914-5084-0 (eBook PDF)
1. Killer whale—Juvenile literature. I. Title.
QL737.C432Z83 2016
599.53′6—dc23 2015006660

Editorial Credits

Brenda Haugen, editor; Kazuko Collins and Juliette Peters, designers; Tracy Cummins, media researcher; Katy LaVigne, production specialist

Photo Credits

Getty Images: Fleetham Dave, 21, Gerard Soury, 15, Greg Johnston, 19; iStockphoto: sethakan, 8; Minden Pictures: Sue Flood, 17; Shutterstock: Doptis, 1, Ferderic B, 2, Back Cover, Monika Wieland, 7, 16, pashabo, Design Element, Tatiana Ivkovich, 3, TOSP, Cover; Thinkstock: Christian Musat, 11, Evgeniya Lazareva, 6, jonmccormackphoto, 5, NicolA!s MeroAo, 13, S_Lew, 12, Tatiana Ivkovich, 9.

Printed in China by Nordica
0415/CA21500544
042015 008845NORDF15

TABLE OF CONTENTS

MIGHTY HUNTERS

Killer whales are deadly **predators**. They roam all the world's oceans. They hunt seals, penguins, fish, and other animals. Killer whales use teamwork and a sharp sense of hearing to find **prey**. Their size and strength help them attack and kill the prey. Killer whales eat as much as 500 pounds (227 kilograms) of food in one day!

FACT

Killer whales are also called orcas.

predator—an animal that hunts other animals for food

prey—an animal hunted by another animal for food

ALL IN THE FAMILY

Killer whales live in family groups called **pods**. A pod may have fewer than five whales to more than 30 whales. Pod members usually work together to find and kill prey. Young killer whales learn to hunt by copying the actions of their older **relatives**.

FACT

A killer whale pod always has a female leader.

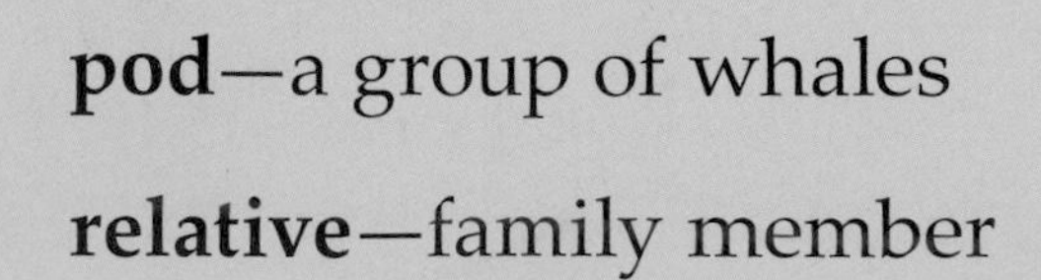

pod—a group of whales

relative—family member

SPEEDY AND STRONG

Killer whales are built for chasing and killing. They have strong, smooth bodies that move through the water quickly. They can swim up to 28 miles (45 km) per hour. Killer whales are also huge. They are bigger and heavier than most cars! Their large size helps them overpower smaller animals.

SEARCHING BY SOUND

Killer whales **communicate** when they hunt together. They make whistles, calls, pops, and jaw claps. These sounds help them hunt as a team. Killer whales also **echolocate**. They click and listen for echoes. From the echoes, killer whales can determine the size, shape, and location of prey.

FACT

Killer whales have no sense of smell.

communicate—to pass along thoughts, feelings, or information

echolocate—to use sounds and echoes to locate objects, such as food

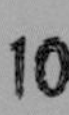

HIDING IN THE OPEN SEA

A killer whale's colors hide it from prey. It can sneak up on prey from above or below it. From above, a killer whale's black back looks like the dark water below. From below, the killer whale's white belly looks like the sunshine above.

FACT

A killer whale's coloring confuses prey. It cannot see the whale's shape clearly.

MANY WAYS TO CATCH A MEAL

Killer whales are clever hunters. They may chase sea **mammals** and trap them in a **bay**. If prey are sitting on sea ice, killer whales bump the ice or make big waves. The killer whales knock the prey into the water, where they can attack. Killer whales also slide onto sea ice and beaches to hunt penguins and seals.

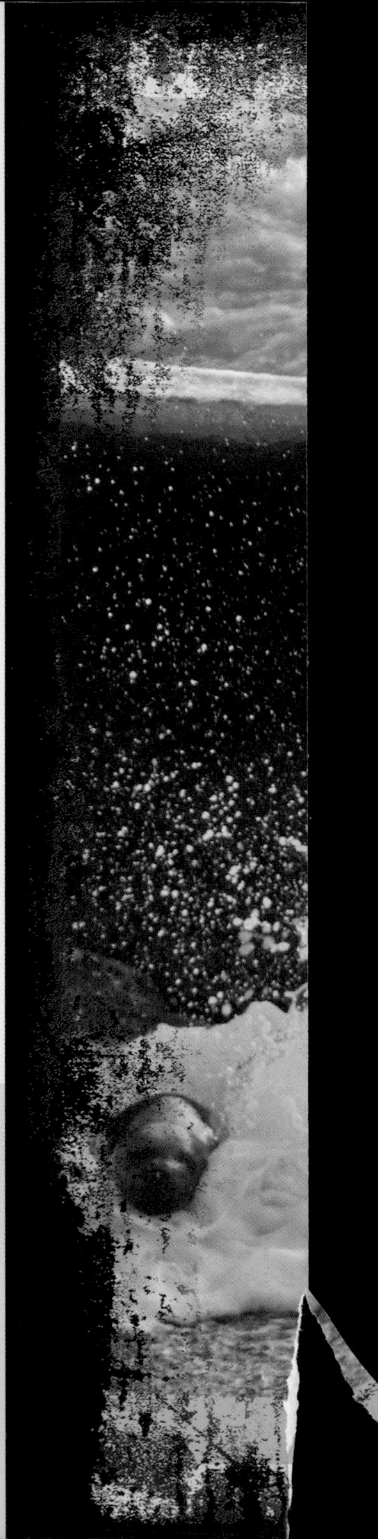

mammal—a warm-blooded animal that breathes air; mammals have hair or fur; female mammals feed milk to their young

bay—a part of the ocean that is partly closed in by land

Killer whales kill prey in different ways. They often circle small prey, such as fish. The whales attack when the fish are trapped. To kill a big whale, killer whales attack it from all sides. Killer whales force sharks to the surface, where the sharks cannot breathe. They hit the sharks with their tails to stun them before eating them.

A pod of killer whales attacks a gray whale.

JAWS OF DEATH

A killer whale's mouth is deadly. Its jaws are big and strong. It has up to 52 pointy teeth. Each tooth is as long as an adult person's finger! The teeth lock together and help the killer whale grip and tear its prey.

FACT

Killer whales are born with all the teeth they will ever have.

LONG LIVE THE KILLER WHALE

Killer whales are deadly hunters that can live a long time. Some killer whales live up to 90 years! Because they are so large, few other animals dare to attack them.

AMAZING BUT TRUE!

A killer whale can never fall completely asleep because it has to think about breathing. Only half of its brain can rest at a time. The other half of the brain stays awake. It helps the killer whale remember to breathe and to watch and listen for danger.

GLOSSARY

bay (BAY)—a part of the ocean that is partly closed in by land

clever (KLEV-er)—having a quick and inventive mind

communicate (kuh-MYOO-nuh-kayt)—to pass along thoughts, feelings, or information

echolocate (eh-koh-LOH-kayt)—to use sounds and echoes to locate objects, such as food

mammal (MAM-uhl)—a warm-blooded animal that breathes air; mammals have hair or fur; female mammals feed milk to their young

pod (POD)—a group of whales

predator (PRED-uh-tur)—an animal that hunts other animals for food

prey (PRAY)—an animal hunted by another animal for food

relative (REL-uh-tiv)—family member

READ MORE

Pallotta, Jerry. *Whale vs. Giant Squid.* Who Would Win? New York: Scholastic, 2012.

Riggs, Kate. *Killer Whales.* Amazing Animals. Mankato, Minn.: Creative Education, 2012.

Weingarten, E. T. *Hunting with Killer Whales.* Animal Attack! New York: Gareth Stevens Publishing, 2014.

INTERNET SITES

FactHound offers a safe, fun way to find Internet sites related to this book. All of the sites on FactHound have been researched by our staff.

Here's all you do:

Visit *www.facthound.com*

Type in this code: 9781491450420

CRITICAL THINKING USING THE COMMON CORE

1. How many teeth does a killer whale have? How do they use their teeth when hunting prey? (Key Ideas and Details)
2. What senses do killer whales use to hunt for prey? Which sense do you think it would be the hardest to go without? Why? (Craft and Structure)

INDEX